Adapted Reading and Study

From Bacteria to Plants

PRENTICE HALL Science Explorer

PEARSON

Prentice
Hall

Boston, Massachusetts
Upper Saddle River, New Jersey

ISBN 0-13-166539-1
7 8 9 10   09

From Bacteria to Plants

Chapter 1 Living Things

Chapter 2 Viruses and Bacteria

Chapter 3 Protists and Fungi

Chapter 4 Introduction to Plants

Chapter 5 Seed Plants

Living Things

What Is Life? (pages 6–14)

The Characteristics of Living Things
(pages 7–9)

Key Concept: **All living things have a cellular organization, contain similar chemicals, use energy, respond to their surroundings, grow and develop, and reproduce.**

- An **organism** is a living thing. You are an organism. So are trees and ants.

- A **cell** is the building block of structures in an organism. **Unicellular** organisms are made of only one cell. **Multicellular** organisms are made of many cells.

- Living things react to what happens around them. A **stimulus** is a change in an organism's surroundings. Light is a stimulus. A **response** is an action or behavior an organism takes when it reacts to a stimulus. A plant bending toward light is a response.

- Living things grow and develop. When a living thing grows, it gets larger. **Development** produces a more complex organism. When organisms grow and develop, their cells use energy to make new cells.

- Living things produce offspring like the parents.

Answer the following questions. Use your textbook and the ideas above.

1. Circle the letter of the building block of structures in all living things.
   a. stimulus
   b. organism
   c. cell

Living Things

2. The picture shows a plant growing toward light. What is the stimulus? _____.

3. Is the following sentence true or false? When a living thing develops, it becomes more complex.

_____

Life Comes From Life (pages 10–11)

Key Concept: **Living things arise from living things through reproduction.**

• Four hundred years ago, people thought living things could come from nonliving things. For example, people thought flies could come from rotting meat.

• Francesco Redi set up an experiment to show that rotting meat does not produce flies.

• Louis Pasteur carried out an experiment that showed bacteria could be produced only from bacteria.

• These experiments helped people understand that living things could not come from nonliving things. Living things come only from other living things through reproduction.

Answer the following question. Use your textbook and the ideas on page 5.

4. Circle the letter of each sentence that is true about where living things come from.

   a. Living things can come from nonliving things.

   b. Redi showed that flies do not come from rotting meat.

   c. Pasteur showed that bacteria come from nonliving materials.

The Needs of Living Things (pages 12–14)

Key Concept: **All living things must satisfy their basic needs for food, water, living space, and stable internal conditions.**

- Living things need food to get the energy to live.

- Some living things use the energy from sunlight to make food. Living things that make their own food are **autotrophs** (AW toh trohfs). Plants are autotrophs.

- Living things that cannot make their own food are **heterotrophs** (HET uh roh trohfs). Heterotrophs get energy by feeding on other living things. Animals are heterotrophs.

- Living things must have water to live. Water dissolves body chemicals and carries the chemicals through the body.

- All living things need a place to live. Living things must get food, water, and shelter from where they live.

- A living thing must be able to keep the conditions inside its body stable, even when conditions around it change. For example, your body temperature stays the same even when the air temperature changes.

Living Things

Answer the following questions. Use your textbook and the ideas on page 6.

5. Read each word in the box. In each sentence below, fill in the correct word.

autotrophs	heterotrophs	organisms

    a. Living things that get energy by feeding on other

        living things are _____.

    b. Living things that use the energy from sunlight to

        make food are _____.

6. Read each word in the box. Use the words to complete the concept map about the needs of living things.

Food	Living space	Sunlight	Water

Living things

need

a. _____

Stable internal conditions

b. _____

c. _____
_____

for   for   for   for

Energy   Dissolving chemicals   Shelter   Cells to work

Classifying Organisms (pages 16–24)

Why Do Scientists Classify? (page 17)

Key Concept: Biologists use classification to organize living things into groups so that the organisms are easier to study.

- Biologists put living things into groups based on how the living things are alike. **Classification** is grouping things based on their similarities.

- The scientific study of how living things are classified is called **taxonomy** (tak SAHN uh mee). Taxonomy is useful because once a living thing is classified, a biologist knows a lot about it. For example, if a crow is classified as a bird, you already know that a crow has feathers and lays eggs.

Answer the following questions. Use your textbook and the ideas above.

1. Read each word in the box. In each sentence below, fill in the correct word.

classification	organization	taxonomy

   a. The scientific study of how living things are classified is called _____.

   b. The grouping of things based on their similarities is called _____.

2. Is the following sentence true or false? It is easier to study living things when they have not been classified.
   _____

Living Things

The Naming System of Linnaeus (pages 18–19)

Key Concept: **Carolus Linnaeus devised a system of naming organisms in which each organism has a unique, two-part scientific name.**

- Linnaeus gave each living thing a scientific name with two parts. The first part of the name is the genus. A **genus** (JEE nus) is a group of similar organisms. For example, all cats belong to the genus *Felis.*

- The second part of a scientific name often describes a distinctive feature of the organism. Together, the two words in a scientific name make up the species. A **species** (SPEE sheez) is a group of similar organisms that can mate and produce offspring that can also mate and reproduce. House cats and lions are in the same genus, but are different species.

- Scientific names make it easier for scientists to talk about organisms. For example, woodchucks are also called groundhogs and whistlepigs. But this animal has only one scientific name—*Marmota monax.*

Answer the following questions. Use your textbook and the ideas above.

3. The scientific name for pumas is *Felis concolor.* Circle the letter of the genus to which pumas belong.
    a. *Felis*
    b. *concolor*
    c. puma

4. Circle the letter of each sentence that is true about scientific names.
    a. Scientific names have two parts.
    b. Organisms in the same species cannot mate and produce offspring.
    c. Scientific names make it easier for scientists to talk about an organism.

Living Things

Levels of Classification (pages 20–21)

Key Concept: **The more classification levels that two organisms share, the more characteristics they have in common.**

- The classification system that scientists use has more groups than just genus and species. Scientists use a series of eight levels to classify organisms. The eight levels are: domain, kingdom, phylum, class, order, family, genus, and species.

- Organisms are grouped by characteristics that they have alike. Organisms with the same classification at lower levels share more characteristics.

- The highest level in the classification system is the domain. The living things in a domain are very wide-ranging. A domain has the largest number of organisms.

- The lowest level in the classification system is the species. The characteristics of a species are very specific. Only one kind of organism is in the species level.

Answer the following questions. Use your textbook and the ideas above.

5. Is the following sentence true or false? Organisms with the same classification at lower levels share more characteristics. _____

6. Circle the letter of the classification level where you would find the most different kinds of organisms.
    a. species
    b. family
    c. domain

Living Things

Taxonomic Keys (page 22)

Key Concept: **Taxonomic keys are useful tools for determining the identity of organisms.**

- Field guides and taxonomic keys are tools that you can use to find out what an organism is.

- A field guide is a book with pictures that show the differences among living things that look similar.

- A taxonomic key has a series of paired statements that describe physical characteristics of a living thing. To use the key, you choose the one statement that applies to the living thing. You continue choosing the one statement of each pair that best describes the living thing. The key leads you to the living thing's identity.

Answer the following questions. Use your textbook and the ideas above.

7. Use the taxonomic key in Figure 14 of your textbook to identify the organism pictured below. Circle the letter of what the organism is.

   a. centipede

   b. spider

   c. scorpion

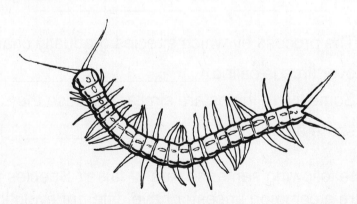

8. A book with pictures that show the differences among similar-looking organisms is a(an)

   _____.

Living Things

Evolution and Classification (pages 23–24)

Key Concept: **Species with similar evolutionary histories are classified more closely together.**

- **Evolution** is the gradual change in species over time.

- Scientists now understand that some living things are similar because they have the same ancestor. For example, the finches on an island and the finches on the mainland both changed little by little from the same species of finch. They became two different species.

- Species that share a common ancestor also share the same evolutionary history. To learn the evolutionary history of a living thing, scientists compare its body structure to other living things. Scientists also compare the chemical makeup of its cells to the cells of other living things.

Answer the following questions. Use your textbook and the ideas above.

9. Read each word in the box. In each sentence below, fill in the correct word.

ancestor	evolution	species

   a. The process by which species gradually change over time is called _____.

   b. Some living things are similar because they share a common _____.

10. Is the following sentence true or false? Species that share a common ancestor have different evolutionary histories. _____

Domains and Kingdoms

(pages 26–29)

Domain Bacteria (page 27)

Key Concept: **Bacteria is one of three domains. Bacteria are unicellular prokaryotes that can be either autotrophs or heterotrophs.**

- Members of the domain Bacteria are single-celled living things.

- Bacteria are prokaryotes. **Prokaryotes** (proh KA ree ohtz) are living things whose cells do not have a nucleus. A **nucleus** (NOO klee us) is a dense area in a cell that holds genetic material.

- Some bacteria make their own food. These bacteria are autotrophic. Other bacteria cannot make their own food. They are heterotrophic.

Answer the following question. Use your textbook and the ideas above.

1. Circle the letter of the best description of members of the domain Bacteria.
   a. are single-celled
   b. are many-celled
   c. have a nucleus

Domain Archaea (page 27)

Key Concept: **Although bacteria and archaea are similar in some ways, there are important differences in the structure and chemical makeup of their cells.**

- Members of the domain Archaea (ahr KEE uh) live in harsh environments like hot springs.

Living Things

- Archaea are single-celled organisms that do not have a nucleus. Some archaea make their own food. Others cannot make their own food.

- Archaea have a different chemical makeup than bacteria have.

Answer the following questions. Use your textbook and the ideas on page 13 and above.

2. Draw lines to show how archaea compare to bacteria.

Archaea	**Characteristic**
like bacteria	**a.** single-celled
	b. do not have nucleus
different from bacteria	**c.** chemical makeup

3. Is the following sentence true or false? All archaea are autotrophs, which make their own food. _____

Domain Eukarya (pages 28–29)

Key Concept: **Scientists classify organisms in the domain Eukarya into one of four kingdoms: protists, fungi, plants, or animals.**

- All members of the domain Eukarya have cells that contain a nucleus. **Eukaryotes** (yoo KA ree ohtz) are living things with cells that have a nucleus.

- Members of the domain Eukarya are classified into one of four kingdoms. These kingdoms are protists, fungi, plants, and animals.

- A protist (PROH tist) is any eukaryote that cannot be classified as a fungi, plant, or animal. Most protists are single-celled.

Living Things

- Fungi (FUN jy) are eukaryotes that cannot make their own food. Most fungi are many-celled.

- Plants are many-celled eukaryotes that can make their own food.

- Animals are many-celled eukaryotes that cannot make their own food.

Answer the following questions. Use your textbook and the ideas on page 14 and above.

4. Circle the letter of the *best* description of all members of the domain Eukarya.
   a. can make their own food
   b. have bodies made of many cells
   c. have cells with a nucleus

5. Fill in the table below about members of the domain Eukarya.

Domain Eukarya		
Kingdom	**Cell Number**	**Able to Make Food?**
Protists	single-celled and many-celled	yes and no
a. _____	single-celled and many-celled	no
Plants	many-celled	b. _____
Animals	c. _____	no

Living Things

The Origin of Life (pages 30–33)

The Atmosphere of Early Earth

(pages 30–31)

Key Concept: On ancient Earth, nitrogen, water vapor, carbon dioxide, and methane were probably the most abundant gases in the atmosphere.

- Scientists think that early Earth was very different than Earth today.

- Today, Earth's atmosphere has mostly the gases nitrogen and oxygen. On early Earth, oxygen was not in the atmosphere.

- Scientists think living things on early Earth were like archaea.

Answer the following questions. Use your textbook and the ideas above.

1. Fill in this Venn diagram to compare the main gases in the atmosphere of early Earth and Earth today.

Early Atmosphere   **Today's Atmosphere**

water vapor

carbon dioxide

a. _____   b. _____   c. _____

2. Is the following sentence true or false? The living things on early Earth were like fungi. _____

Living Things

The First Cells (pages 32–33)

Key Concept: **Scientists hypothesize that the small chemical units of life formed gradually over millions of years in Earth's waters. Some of these chemical units joined to form the large chemical building blocks found in cells. Eventually, some of these large chemicals joined together and became the forerunners of the first cells.**

- Scientists think certain chemicals in early Earth's waters joined to form larger chemicals. Cells formed from these larger chemicals.

- Scientists have found fossils that support their idea about how cells formed. A **fossil** is a trace of an ancient living thing in rock. These fossils look similar to archaea.

- Scientists think the first cells used the chemicals around them for energy. Later, cells formed that could make their own food.

- As the later cells made food, they gave off oxygen. Oxygen built up in Earth's atmosphere for over hundreds of millions of years to reach today's level.

Answer the following question. Use your textbook and the ideas above.

3. Draw a line from each term to its description.

Term	Description
water	**a.** a trace of an ancient living thing
fossil	**b.** where chemicals joined to make the first cells
oxygen	**c.** given off by cells that make their own food

Viruses and Bacteria

Viruses (pages 40–46)

What Is a Virus? (pages 41–42)

Key Concept: **Although viruses can multiply, they do so differently than organisms. Viruses can multiply only when they are inside a living cell.**

- A tiny, nonliving thing that can enter a living cell and reproduce inside the cell is a **virus**.

- Viruses are not living things because viruses are not made of cells. Viruses also cannot make or use food.

- The only way that viruses are like living things is that viruses can make more viruses. But viruses make new viruses only when they are inside a living cell.

- Viruses act like parasites. A **parasite** (PA ruh syt) is an organism that lives on or in a host organism, causing it harm. A **host** is an organism that supplies energy to a virus or another organism. Almost all viruses kill the host cells in which they multiply.

Answer the following questions. Use your textbook and the ideas above.

1. Is the following sentence true or false? A virus is not a living organism because it is not made of cells.

    _____

2. Draw a line from each term to its meaning.

Term	Meaning
virus	**a.** supplies energy to a virus or another organism
parasite	**b.** tiny, nonliving thing that enters a cell to reproduce
host	**c.** lives on or in another organism, causing it harm

Viruses and Bacteria

The Structure of Viruses (page 43)

Key Concept: **All viruses have two basic parts: a protein coat that protects the virus and an inner core made of genetic material.**

- The genetic material in a virus has the instructions for making new viruses.

- The protein coat protects the genetic material. The proteins that make up the coat also help the virus attach to the cells that the virus will infect.

- A virus can infect only certain cells. The virus's protein coat will fit into only certain proteins on the surface of a cell. Not all cells have the proteins that will fit the virus's proteins.

Answer the following questions. Use your textbook and the ideas above.

3. The picture shows the two parts of a virus. Circle the letter of the part that has the instructions for making new viruses.

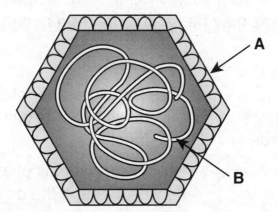

4. Circle the letter of what is NOT a function of the virus's protein coat.

    a. protects genetic material

    b. has instructions for making new viruses

    c. helps a virus attach to the right cell

Viruses and Bacteria

How Viruses Multiply (pages 44–45)

Key Concept: **Once inside a cell, a virus's genetic material takes over many of the cell's functions. It instructs the cell to produce the virus's proteins and genetic material. These proteins and genetic material then assemble into new viruses.**

- Some viruses are active as soon as they enter a cell. The genetic material of an active virus takes over the functions of the cell right away and starts making new viruses. The cell dies when the new viruses burst out.

- Other viruses are not active right away. The virus may stay inactive for years. When conditions are right, the virus's genetic material suddenly becomes active. It takes over the cell's functions and begins making new viruses. When the cell is full of new viruses, the cell bursts open and dies.

Answer the following questions. Use your textbook and the ideas above.

5. Draw a line from each virus to its description. The descriptions may be used more than once.

Virus	Description
active virus	**a.** The virus's genetic material takes over the cell's functions.
hidden virus	**b.** The virus multiplies as soon as it enters the cell.
	c. The virus may stay inactive for a long time.

6. Is the following sentence true or false? A cell does not die when the new viruses leave the cell. _____

Viruses and Bacteria

Viruses and the Living World (page 46)

Key Concept: **Even though viruses cause diseases, they can also be used to treat some diseases.**

- Viruses cause diseases in people and other living things. For example, viruses cause colds and flu in people and rabies in dogs and cats.

- Gene therapy is used to treat some diseases. Scientists add genetic material to a virus. The virus carries the genetic material into the cell that needs it. Scientists have changed the virus so that it will not harm the cell.

Answer the following questions. Use your textbook and the ideas above.

7. Circle the letter of each sentence that is true about viruses.

   a. Viruses cause diseases only in people.

   b. In gene therapy, scientists use a virus to carry genetic material to a cell that needs it.

   c. The viruses used in gene therapy can harm the cell.

8. Is the following sentence true or false? Colds and flu are caused by viruses. _____

Bacteria (pages 48–57)

The Bacterial Cell (pages 48–50)

Key Concept: **Bacteria are prokaryotes. The genetic material in their cells is not contained in a nucleus.**

- **Bacteria** are single-celled organisms that do not have a nucleus.

- The outside of a bacterial cell is usually protected by a stiff cell wall.

- Just inside the cell wall is the cell membrane. The cell membrane controls what can go in and out of the bacterial cell.

- The area inside the cell membrane is the cytoplasm. The **cytoplasm** (SY toh plaz um) is a gel-like material. The cell's genetic material is in the cytoplasm. The genetic material looks like a tangled string.

- Some bacteria have a flagellum attached to the outside of the membrane. A **flagellum** (fluh JEL um) is a long, whiplike structure that helps a cell to move. Bacteria without a flagellum are carried by the wind or water.

Answer the following questions. Use your textbook and the ideas above.

1. The picture shows different parts of a bacterial cell.

    a. Circle the letter of the cytoplasm.

    b. Underline the letter of a flagellum.

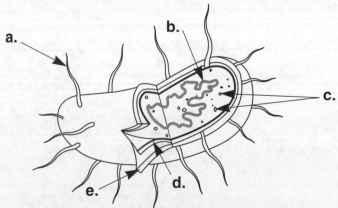

Viruses and Bacteria

2. Is the following sentence true or false? Bacteria are living things made up of many cells. _____

Obtaining Food and Energy (pages 50–51)

***Key Concept:* Bacteria must have a source of food and a way of breaking down the food to release its energy.**

- Bacteria need energy to live. This energy comes from food.

- Some bacteria can make their own food. Autotrophic bacteria either use energy from the sun or chemicals in the environment to make food.

- Other bacteria cannot make their own food. Heterotrophic bacteria get food by eating other organisms or the food made by other organisms.

- Breaking down food to release its energy is called **respiration**.

Answer the following question. Use your textbook and the ideas above.

3. Read each word in the box. In each sentence below, fill in the correct word.

autotrophic	energy	heterotrophic
respiration		

   a. Bacteria that use energy from the sun to make food are _____.

   b. The process of breaking down food to release its energy is called _____.

   c. To carry out their functions, bacteria need a constant supply of _____.

Viruses and Bacteria

Reproduction (pages 52–53)

Key Concept: **When bacteria have plenty of food, the right temperature, and other suitable conditions, they thrive and reproduce frequently.**

- Bacteria reproduce in the right conditions. The right conditions include plenty of food and water and the right temperature.

- Bacteria reproduce by binary fission. In **binary fission**, one cell divides to form two identical cells.

- Binary fission is a form of asexual reproduction. **Asexual reproduction** involves only one parent. The parent produces offspring that are identical to it.

- Sometimes bacteria undergo conjugation. In **conjugation** (kahn juh GAY shun), one bacterial cell transfers some genetic material into another bacterial cell.

- Conjugation is a form of sexual reproduction. **Sexual reproduction** involves two parents. The offspring of sexual reproduction are genetically different from either parent.

Answer the following questions. Use your textbook and the ideas above.

4. Circle the letter of when bacteria will reproduce.
    a. when there is no food
    b. only when water dries up
    c. when there is plenty of food and the temperature is right

Viruses and Bacteria

5. Read each word in the box. Use the words to complete the concept map about reproduction in bacteria.

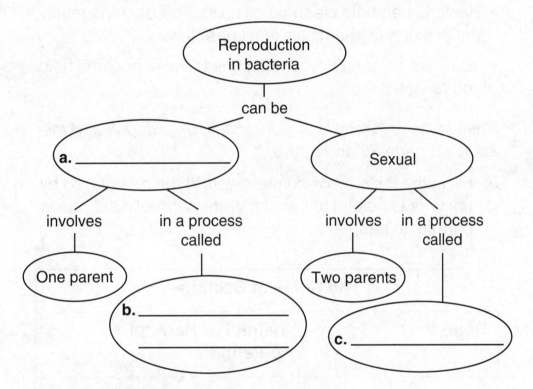

```
┌─────────────────────────────────────────────────┐
│  Asexual        Binary fission    Conjugation     │
│  Reproduction                                     │
└─────────────────────────────────────────────────┘
```

The Role of Bacteria in Nature (pages 54–57)

Key Concept: **Bacteria are involved in oxygen and food production, environmental recycling and cleanup, and in health maintenance and medicine production.**

• You might think that bacteria are only harmful because they cause disease. However, most bacteria are harmless. Some are even helpful to people.

• When bacteria make food with the sun's energy, they release oxygen into the air. These bacteria help keep the right amount of oxygen in the air.

Viruses and Bacteria

- Foods like vinegar, yogurt, and cheeses are made with the help of bacteria. Other kinds of bacteria cause food to spoil. Eating spoiled food can make you sick.

- Some bacteria break down the chemicals in dead organisms. Plants use these broken down chemicals to grow.

- Bacteria can help clean up oil spills. The bacteria make the poisonous chemicals in oil harmless.

- You have bacteria in your intestines. These bacteria help you to digest food.

Answer the following question. Use your textbook and the ideas on page 25 and above.

6. Fill in the table below. Write *helpful* if the role played by bacteria is helpful to people. Write *harmful* if the role is harmful to people.

The Roles of Bacteria	
Role	**Helpful or Harmful to People?**
Cause diseases	a. _____
Give off oxygen	b. _____
Used to make foods	c. _____
Spoil foods	d. _____
Break down dead organisms	e. _____
Clean up oil spills	f. _____

Viruses and Bacteria

Viruses, Bacteria, and Your Health (pages 60–65)

How Infectious Diseases Spread (pages 60–61)

Key Concept: **Infectious diseases can spread through contact with an infected person, a contaminated object, an infected animal, or an environmental source.**

- An **infectious disease** is an illness that passes from one organism to another. Colds are infectious diseases.

- Disease-causing viruses or bacteria infect a person by entering breaks in the skin. Viruses and bacteria may also be breathed in or swallowed.

- Direct contact with an infected person can spread an infectious disease. Touching a person is direct contact.

- Touching objects that were handled by an infected person can spread infectious diseases. For example, drinking from the same cup as an infected person spreads a cold.

- Animal bites can spread infectious diseases. Some infectious diseases are spread by ticks and mosquitoes.

- Some disease-causing viruses and bacteria live in food, soil, and water. Eating foods or drinking water without first killing the bacteria can make you sick.

Answer the following questions. Use your textbook and the ideas above.

1. An illness that passes from one organism to another is a(an) _____.

2. Is the following sentence true or false? You cannot swallow or breath in viruses or bacteria that cause disease. _____

Viruses and Bacteria

3. Fill in the concept map about how infectious diseases are spread.

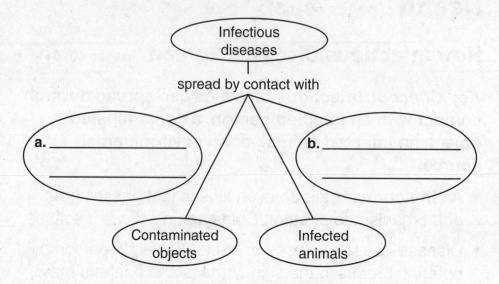

Treating Infectious Diseases (pages 62–64)

Key Concept: **Many bacterial diseases can be cured with medications known as antibiotics. Currently, no medications can cure viral infections.**

- Many diseases caused by bacteria can be treated and cured with antibiotics. An **antibiotic** is a chemical that kills bacteria without harming a person.

- Diseases caused by viruses cannot be cured with medicines. The best treatment for a disease caused by a virus is resting, drinking lots of fluids, and eating balanced meals.

Answer the following questions. Use your textbook and the ideas above.

4. Many diseases caused by bacteria can be cured

   with _____.

5. Resting and drinking lots of fluids is the best treatment

   for diseases caused by _____.

Viruses and Bacteria

Preventing Infectious Diseases (page 65)

Key Concept: **Vaccines are important tools that help prevent the spread of infectious diseases.**

- One of the best ways to keep from getting a disease is by getting a vaccine. A **vaccine** causes the body to produce chemicals that destroy certain viruses or bacteria.

- Keeping your body healthy prevents disease. Eat healthful foods. Get enough sleep. Drink lots of fluids.

- Keeping clean also prevents disease. Wash your hands. Do not share cups. Keep the kitchen clean.

- When you are sick, do not spread your disease to other people. Cover your mouth when you cough or sneeze. Wash your hands often.

Answer the following questions. Use your textbook and the ideas above.

6. If you wanted your body to produce chemicals that destroy certain viruses or bacteria, you would get a(an)

   _____.

7. Circle the picture that shows a way to keep from spreading infectious diseases.

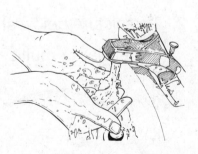

Protists and Fungi

Protists (pages 74–83)

What Is a Protist? (page 75)

Key Concept: **Protists are eukaryotes that cannot be classified as animals, plants, or fungi.**

• **Protists** are eukaryotes, or living things whose cells have a nucleus. Any eukaryote that is not classified as an animal, plant, or fungus is classified as a protist.

• All protists live in moist places.

• Most protists are unicellular—just one cell. Some protists are multicellular—made up of many cells.

• Some protists can move. Others cannot move.

• Scientists group protists based on the characteristics they share with animals, plants, or fungi.

Answer the following questions. Use your textbook and the ideas above.

1. Circle the letter of each sentence that is true about protists.

   a. Protists, like bacteria, do not have a nucleus in their cells.

   b. All protists live in moist places.

   c. All protists can move.

2. The picture below shows a protist. Is this protist unicellular or multicellular? _____

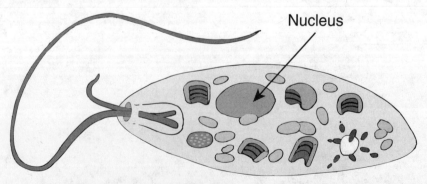

Nucleus

Protists and Fungi

Animal-Like Protists (pages 75–78)

Key Concept: **Like animals, animal-like protists are heterotrophs, and most are able to move from place to place to obtain food.**

- Animal-like protists are called protozoans. **Protozoans** (proh tuh ZOH unz) are single-celled eukaryotes that cannot make their own food. Most protozoans move to get food. Eukaryotes are living things with a nucleus in their cells.

- Some protozoans get food by forming pseudopods. **Pseudopods** (SOO duh pahdz) are temporary bulges of the cell. Pseudopods form when cytoplasm flows toward one direction and the rest of the organism follows.

- Other protozoans have cilia. **Cilia** (SIL ee uh) are hairlike structures that move with a wavelike motion. Cilia act like tiny oars to move an organism. Cilia also sweep food into the organism.

- Another group of protozoans use long, whiplike flagella to move.

Answer the following questions. Use your textbook and the ideas above.

3. Circle the letter of a single-celled eukaryote that cannot make its own food.

   a. bacteria   **b.** virus   **c.** protozoan

4. The pictures show two different protozoans. Circle the picture of the protozoan that has cilia.

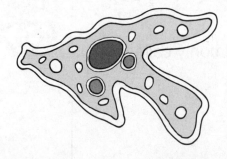 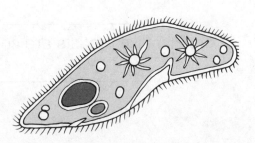

Protists and Fungi

Plantlike Protists (pages 79–81)

***Key Concept:* Like plants, algae are autotrophs.**

- **Algae** (AL jee) are protists that use the sun's energy to make their own food. Autotrophs are living things that can make their own food.

- Some algae are unicellular. Other algae are multicellular.

- Algae can be green, yellow, red, brown, orange, or black. Algae have these different colors because algae contain pigments. **Pigments** are chemicals that produce color.

- Scientists have divided algae into different groups based on their color and structure.

Answer the following questions. Use your textbook and the ideas above.

5. Is the following sentence true or false? All plantlike protists are unicellular. _____

6. Read each word in the box. In each sentence below, fill in the correct word.

algae	autotrophs	pigments	protozoans

   a. Because plantlike protists can make their own food, they are _____.

   b. Chemicals that produce color are called

   _____.

   c. Plantlike protists are commonly called

   _____.

Name _____ Date _____ Class _____

Protists and Fungi

Funguslike Protists (pages 82–83)

Key Concept: **Like fungi, funguslike protists are heterotrophs, have cells walls, and use spores to reproduce.**

- Funguslike protists cannot make their food. Heterotrophs are living things that cannot make their own food.

- Funguslike protists have cell walls. Cell walls make cells very stiff. Plant cells also have cell walls.

- Funguslike protists use spores to reproduce. A **spore** is a tiny cell that grows into a new organism.

- All funguslike protists can move at some point in their lives.

Answer the following questions. Use your textbook and the ideas above.

7. Circle the letter of each characteristic of funguslike protists.
    a. cannot make their own food
    b. have cell walls
    c. cannot move at all

8. A tiny cell that grows into a new organism is a(an)

    _____.

Algal Blooms (pages 84–86)

Saltwater Blooms (page 85)

Key Concept: **Algal blooms occur when nutrients increase in the water. Red tides are dangerous when the toxins that the algae produce become concentrated in the bodies of organisms that consume the algae.**

- An **algal bloom** is the rapid growth of algae.

- **Red tides** are algal blooms in salt water. Not all red tides look red. The color depends on the species of algae that blooms.

- Red tides seem to be caused by warmer water temperatures and more nutrients in the water.

- Red tides are dangerous because the algae produce poisons. When animals eat the algae, the animals store the poisons in their bodies. People and other animals that eat those animals can get sick from the stored poisons.

Answer the following questions. Use your textbook and the ideas above.

1. The rapid growth of algae is called a(an)

   _____.

2. Circle the letter of each sentence that is true about red tides.

   a. A red tide is a rapid growth of algae in salt water.
   b. One cause of red tides is less nutrients in the water.
   c. Red tides are dangerous to people and other animals.

Protists and Fungi

Freshwater Blooms (page 86)

Key Concept: **Eutrophication triggers a series of events with serious consequences.**

- **Eutrophication** (yoo troh fih KAY shun) is when nutrients build up in a lake or pond over time, causing more algae to grow.

- Extra nutrients in a lake can cause an algal bloom.

- An algal bloom in a lake or pond keeps sunlight from reaching plants in the water. The plants die and sink to the bottom. Bacteria that break down the dead plants multiply in the water. The bacteria use up all the oxygen in the water. Then the fish and other organisms in the water die. Only the algae on the water's surface are alive.

Answer the following question. Use your textbook and the ideas above.

3. Read the flowchart. Fill in the missing words.

Eutrophication

┌───┐
│   │
│   Too many nutrients flow into a lake.   │
│   │
└───┘
                              │
                              ▼
┌───┐
│ Algal bloom keeps **a.** _____   │
│   │
│ from reaching plants in the water. The plants die.   │
└───┘
                              │
                              ▼
┌───┐
│ Bacteria break down dead plants. Soon the bacteria use up all the │
│   │
│ **b.** _____ in the water.   │
└───┘
                              │
                              ▼
┌───┐
│   │
│   Fishes and other organisms in the water die.   │
│   │
└───┘

Protists and Fungi

Fungi (pages 88–95)

What Are Fungi? (pages 88–90)

Key Concept: **Fungi are eukaryotes that have cell walls, are heterotrophs that feed by absorbing their food, and use spores to reproduce.**

- **Fungi** are living things that cannot make their own food. Fungi have cells with a nucleus and a cell wall.

- Fungi grow in warm, moist places.

- Fungi can be single-celled or many-celled. Many-celled fungi have cells arranged in structures called hyphae. **Hyphae** (HY fee) are branching, threadlike tubes that make up the body of fungi.

- Fungi do not take food inside their bodies. Hyphae ooze chemicals that break down their food. Then the hyphae absorb the smaller food particles.

Answer the following questions. Use your textbook and the ideas above.

1. Circle the letter of how fungi get food.

   a. Hyphae sweep bits of food into the cells.

   b. Hyphae make food using the sun's energy.

   c. Hyphae ooze chemicals that break down food.

2. The picture shows the structures of a mushroom. Draw arrows that point to hyphae.

Protists and Fungi

Reproduction in Fungi (pages 90–91)

Key Concept: **Fungi usually reproduce by making spores. The lightweight spores are surrounded by a protective covering and can be carried easily through air or water to new sites.**

- Fungi reproduce asexually when there is enough food and water. In asexual reproduction, cells at the tips of the hyphae divide to form spores. The spores grow into fungi that are identical to the parent.

- Fungi produce millions of spores. Wind and water carry spores to new places. Only a few spores fall in places where they can grow.

- Fungi reproduce sexually when there is not much food and water. In sexual reproduction, hyphae from two fungi grow together. Then the fungi trade genetic material. A new structure grows from the joined hyphae and makes spores. The spores grow into fungi that are different from either parent.

Answer the following questions. Use your textbook and the ideas above.

3. Draw a line from each type of reproduction to its description. The descriptions can be used more than once.

Type of Reproduction	Description
asexual	a. produces spores
sexual	b. offspring different from parents
	c. offspring identical to parent

4. Is the following sentence true or false? All spores produced by a fungus grow into new fungi. _____

Name _____ Date _____ Class _____

Protists and Fungi

The Role of Fungi in Nature (pages 92–95)

Key Concept: Fungi play important roles as decomposers and recyclers on Earth. Many fungi provide foods for people. Some fungi cause disease while others fight disease. Still other fungi live in symbiosis with other organisms.

• Many fungi break down the chemicals in dead organisms. This process returns nutrients to the soil.

• Yeast is a fungus used to make bread and wine. Molds are used to make cheeses. Mushrooms are eaten in salads and on pizza.

• Some molds produce chemicals that kill bacteria. Penicillin is an antibiotic that is made from a mold.

• Some fungi cause disease in plants and animals. Dutch elm disease is a fungus that has killed millions of elm trees.

• Some fungi grow around plant roots. Their hyphae absorb nutrients and water for the plant. The fungus feeds on extra food stored in the plant's roots.

• Fungi that grow together with certain algae or bacteria form an organism called a **lichen** (LY kun). Lichens are flat, crusty patches that grow on tree bark or rocks. The fungus gets food made by the algae or bacteria. The algae or bacteria get shelter, water, and minerals from the fungus.

Answer the following question. Use your textbook and the ideas above.

5. Circle the letter of each sentence that is true about the roles of fungi.
    a. A fungus is used to make bread and wine.
    b. Fungi do not cause any diseases in people.
    c. Fungi help some plants by growing on their roots.

Introduction to Plants

The Plant Kingdom (pages 104–111)

What Is a Plant? (pages 104–105)

Key Concept: **Nearly all plants are autotrophs, organisms that produce their own food. All plants are eukaryotes that contain many cells. In addition, all plant cells are surrounded by cell walls.**

- Plants make their own food in a process called **photosynthesis**. In photosynthesis, a plant uses carbon dioxide gas and water to make food.

- All plants are made up of many cells. The cells in a plant are organized into tissues. **Tissues** are groups of cells that have a specific job. For example, many plants have tissues that move water through their bodies.

- All plant cells have a nucleus and a stiff cell wall.

- All plant cells have chloroplasts. **Chloroplasts** (KLAWR uh plasts) are the structures in which food is made.

Answer the following questions. Use your textbook and the ideas above.

1. Draw a line from each term to its meaning.

Term	Meaning
photosynthesis	a. structure in a plant cell in which food is made
tissue	b. a group of cells that have a specific job
chloroplast	c. the process in which plants make food

Introduction to Plants

2. The picture shows a plant cell. Circle the letter of the
   cell structure that is the cell wall.

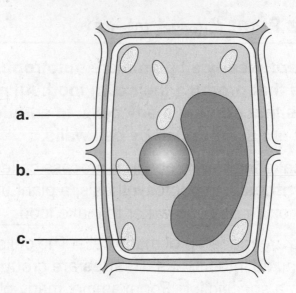

a.

b.

c.

Adaptations for Living on Land
(pages 106–107)

Key Concept: **For plants to survive on land, they must
have ways to obtain water and other nutrients from
their surroundings, retain water, transport materials in
their bodies, support their bodies, and reproduce.**

• Plant leaves can easily lose water to the air. To keep
  from losing water, most plant leaves are covered with a
  cuticle. A **cuticle** is a waxy, waterproof layer of a leaf.

• Plants move water, nutrients, and wastes through their
  bodies. Large plants have tissues that move these
  materials. **Vascular tissue** is a system of tubes inside a
  plant that water and food move through.

• Large and tall plants need support to hold their leaves
  up to the sun. Stiff cell walls and vascular tissue
  strengthen and support the large bodies of these plants.

• All plants reproduce by sexual reproduction. In the
  process of **fertilization**, a sperm cell from the male
  parent joins with an egg cell from the female parent. The
  fertilized egg cell is called a **zygote**.

Introduction to Plants

Answer the following questions. Use your textbook and the ideas on page 40.

3. Circle the letter of each sentence that is true about plants.

    a. The cuticle helps support tall plants.

    b. Water and food move through vascular tissue.

    c. All plants reproduce by sexual reproduction.

4. Read each word in the box. In each sentence below, fill in the correct word.

fertilization	photosynthesis	zygote

    a. A fertilized egg cell is called a

    _____.

    b. A sperm cell joins with an egg cell in the

    process of _____.

Classification of Plants (pages 108–110)

Key Concept: **Scientists informally group plants into two major groups—nonvascular plants and vascular plants.**

- **Nonvascular plants** are plants that do not have a system of tubes for moving water and food.

- Nonvascular plants are low-growing plants. They also do not have true roots, stems, or leaves. These plants get water directly from their surroundings. Nonvascular plants grow in damp, shady places.

- **Vascular plants** have a system of tubes for moving water and food. Vascular plants can grow very tall because vascular tissue also gives the plant support.

Introduction to Plants

Answer the following questions. Use your textbook and the ideas on page 41.

5. Plants that do not have a system of tubes for moving water and food are called _____ plants.

6. Fill in the table about the two major groups of plants.

Classification of Plants		
Group	**Vascular System**	**Size**
Nonvascular	**a.** _____	short
Vascular	yes	**b.** _____

Complex Life Cycles (pages 110–111)

***Key Concept:* Plants have complex life cycles that include two different stages, the sporophyte stage and the gametophyte stage.**

• In the **sporophyte** (SPOH ruh fyt) stage, the plant produces spores. Spores are tiny cells that can grow into new organisms.

• A spore grows and develops to become the gametophyte. In the **gametophyte** (guh MEE tuh fyt) stage, the plant produces two kinds of sex cells: sperm cells and egg cells.

• When a sperm cell and egg cell join, they form a zygote. The zygote grows and develops into a sporophyte. The sporophyte produces spores, which grow into gametophytes. The gametophyte produces sperm cells and egg cells. And the cycle begins again.

Introduction to Plants

Answer the following question. Use your textbook and the ideas on page 42.

7. Read each word in the box. Use the words to complete the cycle diagram about the plant life cycle.

| gametophyte | spores | sporophyte | zygote |

Plant Life Cycle

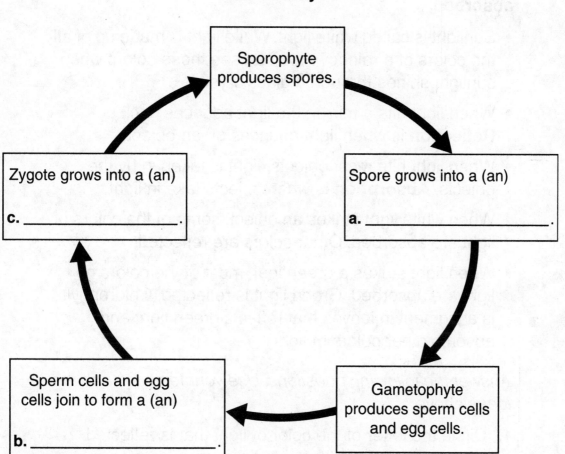

Introduction to Plants

Photosynthesis and Light

(pages 114–119)

The Nature of Light (pages 115–116)

Key Concept: **When light strikes the green leaves of a plant, most of the green part of the spectrum is reflected. Most of the other colors of light are absorbed.**

- Sunlight is called white light. White light is made up of all the colors of a rainbow. You can see these colors when sunlight shines through a glass crystal.

- When light hits a mirror, the light bounces back. **Reflection** is when light bounces off an object.

- When light hits most objects, light is taken in by the objects. **Absorption** is when objects take in light.

- When white light strikes an object, some of the colors of light are absorbed. Other colors are reflected.

- When light strikes a green leaf, most of the colors of light are absorbed. Green light is reflected. Chlorophyll is a pigment in leaves that reflects green light and absorbs other colors of light.

Answer the following questions. Use your textbook and the ideas above.

1. Circle the letter of the color of light that is reflected when white light strikes green leaves.
   a. red
   b. green
   c. blue

Introduction to Plants

2. Read each word in the box. In each sentence below, fill in the correct word or words.

> absorption   reflection   white light

    a. When light hits an object and that object takes in the light, it is called _____.

    b. When light hits an object and bounces off, it is called _____.

The Photosynthesis Process (pages 117–119)

Key Concept: **The many chemical reactions of photosynthesis can be summarized by this equation:**

$$\text{carbon dioxide} + \text{water} \xrightarrow{\text{light energy}} \text{sugar} + \text{oxygen}$$

- When light strikes a leaf, the two-part process of photosynthesis begins.

- In the first part of photosynthesis, the green pigment chlorophyll absorbs energy from sunlight.

- Plants use the energy from sunlight to power a series of chemical reactions. In these reactions, carbon dioxide gas from air and water from soil combine. These reactions produce sugar and oxygen gas.

- The food (sugar) made during photosynthesis gives the plant the energy it needs. Extra food is stored in the roots, stems, leaves, or fruit.

- Oxygen made during photosynthesis goes into the air. Other living things use this oxygen.

Introduction to Plants

Answer the following questions. Use your textbook and the ideas on page 45.

3. The picture shows a plant and some materials of photosynthesis.

   a. For materials that a plant takes in for photosynthesis, draw arrows that point to the plant.

   b. For materials the plant gives off in photosynthesis, draw arrows that point away from the plant.

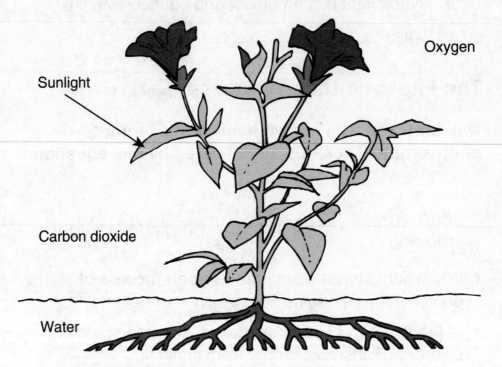

Sunlight

Oxygen

Carbon dioxide

Water

4. Is the following sentence true or false? Extra food made by plants can be stored in the roots, stems, leaves, or fruit. _____

Mosses, Liverworts, and Hornworts (pages 122–124)

Mosses (page 123)

***Key Concept:* Mosses are one group of nonvascular plants. Mosses are low-growing plants that live in moist environments where they can absorb water and other nutrients directly from their environment.**

- Mosses need a moist place to live so that sperm cells can swim to egg cells for reproduction. Mosses also absorb water and nutrients directly into their cells.

- The green, fuzzy part of a moss plant is the gametophyte stage. The gametophyte is low-growing. It has structures that look like roots, stems, and leaves.

- The sporophyte stage grows out of the gametophyte. The sporophyte is a long, thin stalk. A capsule at the end of the stalk makes spores.

Answer the following questions. Use your textbook and the ideas above.

1. Why do mosses need a moist home? Circle the letter of the correct answer.
   a. They can grow taller.
   b. Their spores can spread.
   c. They can reproduce.

2. The picture shows a moss plant. Identify the gametophyte stage and the sporophyte stage of the plant.

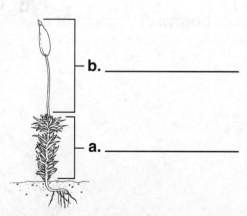

b. _____

a. _____

Name _____ Date _____ Class _____

Introduction to Plants

Liverworts and Hornworts (page 124)

Key Concept: **Liverworts and hornworts are two groups of nonvascular plants. These low-growing plants live in moist environments where they can absorb water and other nutrients directly from their environment.**

- Liverworts have sporophytes that are too small to see. The gametophytes are leaflike structures shaped like a human liver.

- Liverworts often grow as a thick crust on moist rocks or soil along a stream.

- Hornworts have gametophytes that lie flat on the ground. The sporophytes are slender, curved structures that look like horns growing out of the gametophyte.

- Hornworts usually grow in moist soil, often mixed in with grass plants.

Answer the following question. Use your textbook and the ideas above.

3. Draw a line from each nonvascular plant to its description. The plants may have more than one description.

Nonvascular Plant

liverwort

hornwort

Description

a. Sporophytes look like horns.

b. Gametophytes are shaped like a human liver.

c. Grows on moist rocks or along streams.

d. Grows in moist soil mixed with grass plants.

Ferns, Club Mosses, and Horsetails (pages 126–129)

Characteristics of Seedless Vascular Plants (page 127)

Key Concept: **Seedless vascular plants have true vascular tissue and they do not produce seeds. Instead of seeds, these plants reproduce by releasing spores.**

- Vascular plants are tall because vascular tissue easily moves food and water through the plant. Vascular tissue also supports the plant.

- Seedless vascular plants must grow in moist places. Seedless vascular plants release spores. The spores grow into gametophytes. When the gametophytes produce sperm cells and egg cells, there must be enough water for the sperm to swim to the eggs.

Answer the following questions. Use your textbook and the ideas above.

1. Circle the letter of each sentence that is true about vascular plants.

    a. Vascular plants are short so that food and water can move through them more easily.

    b. Vascular tissue gives plants support.

    c. Seedless vascular plants need water to reproduce.

2. Seedless vascular plants produce spores that grow into _____.

Introduction to Plants

Ferns (page 128)

***Key Concept:* Ferns are one group of seedless vascular plants.**

- Ferns have true stems, roots, and leaves. Most ferns have underground stems. Roots anchor a fern to the ground and absorb water and nutrients from the soil.

- Fern leaves, or **fronds**, are divided into many smaller parts.

- A fern plant with fronds is the sporophyte stage of the plant. Spores develop on the undersides of fronds. Wind and water carry the spores away.

- If a spore lands in moist, shaded soil, the spore develops into a gametophyte. Fern gametophytes are tiny plants that grow low to the ground.

Answer the following questions. Use your textbook and the ideas above.

3. The picture shows a fern plant. Circle a frond.

4. Is the following sentence true or false? A fern plant with fronds is the gametophyte stage of the plant.

_____

Introduction to Plants

Club Mosses and Horsetails (page 129)

Key Concept: **Club mosses and horsetails are two groups of seedless vascular plants.**

- The life cycle of club mosses and horsetails is similar to the fern life cycle. The plant you see is a sporophyte. The sporophyte produces spores.

- Club mosses and horsetails have vascular tissue.

- Club mosses look like tiny pine trees. They usually grow in moist woods and near streams.

- Horsetails have jointed stems. Needlelike branches and small leaves grow in a circle around each joint.

Answer the following question. Use your textbook and the ideas above.

5. Read each word in the box. Use the words to complete the Venn diagram about club mosses and horsetails.

nonvascular   seeds   spores   vascular

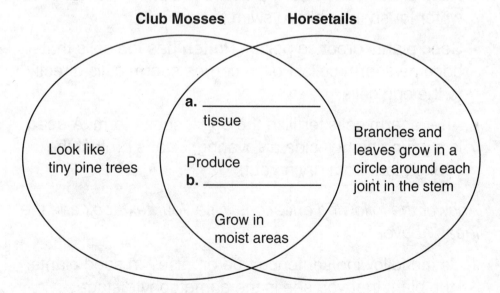

Club Mosses   **Horsetails**

Look like tiny pine trees

a. _____ tissue

Produce
b. _____

Grow in moist areas

Branches and leaves grow in a circle around each joint in the stem

Name _____ Date _____ Class _____

Seed Plants

The Characteristics of Seed Plants (pages 136–145)

What Is a Seed Plant? (pages 136–137)

Key Concept: **Seed plants share two important characteristics. They have vascular tissue, and they use pollen and seeds to reproduce.**

- All seed plants have roots, stems, and leaves.

- In seed plants, the plant that you see is the sporophyte stage of the plant. The gametophyte stage is very small.

- Seed plants have vascular tissue. There are two kinds of vascular tissue:
    1. **Phloem** (FLOH um) is the vascular tissue that food moves through. Food is the sugar made in the leaves during photosynthesis.
    2. **Xylem** (ZY lum) is the vascular tissue that water moves through. The roots take up water from the soil.

- Seed plants can live any place. Seed plants do not need water for sperm cells to swim to egg cells.

- Seed plants produce pollen. **Pollen** has the cells that become sperm cells. Pollen carries sperm cells directly to the egg cells.

- After sperm cells fertilize the eggs, seeds form. A **seed** is a young plant inside a covering. Seeds protect the young plant from drying out.

Answer the following questions. Use your textbook and the ideas above.

1. Is the following sentence true or false? In seed plants, the plant that you see is the gametophyte stage.

_____

2. Draw a line from each term to its meaning.

Term	Meaning
phloem	**a.** a young plant inside a protective covering
xylem	**b.** vascular tissue that water moves through
pollen	**c.** vascular tissue that food moves through
seed	**d.** structure that carries sperm cells to egg cells

How Seeds Become New Plants

(pages 138–140)

Key Concept: **Inside a seed is a partially developed plant. If a seed lands in an area where conditions are favorable, the plant sprouts out of the seed and begins to grow.**

• A seed holds a young plant that has tiny roots, stems, and leaves. The young plant also has seed leaves called **cotyledons** (kaht uh LEED unz). In some seeds, the cotyledons have stored food.

• The outer covering of a seed is called the seed coat. The seed coat keeps the young plant from drying out.

• After seeds form, they are scattered far from the plant. Seeds are scattered by animals, water, and wind.

• After a seed is scattered, the seed stays inactive until it absorbs water. **Germination** (jur muh NAY shun) occurs when the young plant begins to grow and pushes out of the seed. The young plant uses stored food to grow.

Name _____ Date _____ Class _____

Seed Plants

Answer the following questions. Use your textbook and the ideas on page 53.

3. Read each word in the box. In each sentence below, fill in the correct word or words.

cotyledon germination seed coat

   a. A seed leaf inside the seed is a

     _____.

   b. When a plant begins to grow and pushes out of the

     seed, the process is called _____.

4. Fill in the concept map to show ways that seeds are scattered.

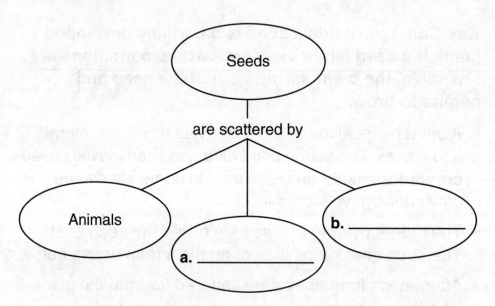

5. Circle the letter of each sentence that is true about seeds becoming new plants.

   a. The seed coat keeps the young plant from drying out.

   b. After seeds are scattered, they germinate right away.

   c. The young plant uses stored food to grow.

Name _____ Date _____ Class _____

Seed Plants

Roots (pages 140–141)

Key Concept: **Roots anchor a plant in the ground, absorb water and minerals from the soil, and sometimes store food.**

- Plants have two kinds of root systems:
  1. A fibrous root system has many roots of the same size. Grass has fibrous roots.
  2. A taproot root system has one long main root. Smaller roots branch off the main root. Carrots have taproots.

- Root hairs grow out of a root's surface. Root hairs absorb water and minerals from the soil. Root hairs also help hold a plant in the soil.

- Xylem in the roots moves water and minerals from the soil up to the stems and leaves.

- Phloem moves food that was made in the leaves down to the roots. Roots use the energy from food to grow. Extra food is sometimes stored in roots.

Answer the following questions. Use your textbook and the ideas above.

6. The picture shows two plants with different kinds of root systems. Circle the letter of the plant with a taproot root system.

a.

b.

Seed Plants

7. Draw a line from each term to its function in a root.

Term	Function
root hairs	**a.** moves water and minerals to the leaves
xylem	**b.** anchor the plant and absorb water and minerals
phloem	**c.** moves food into the roots

Stems (pages 142–143)

Key Concept: **The stem carries substances between the plant's roots and leaves. The stem also provides support for the plant and holds up the leaves so they are exposed to the sun.**

- A stem has two main jobs:
  1. The stem moves food and water between the roots and the leaves.
  2. The stem also supports the plant and holds up leaves to the light.

- Stems can be herbaceous (hur BAY shus) or woody. Herbaceous stems are soft and green. Tomato plants have herbaceous stems. Woody stems are hard and stiff. Trees have woody stems.

Answer the following questions. Use your textbook and the ideas above.

8. Circle the letter of each job of a stem.
   a. moving water between the roots and leaves
   b. supporting the plant
   c. absorbing water from the soil

9. Is the following sentence true or false? Woody

   stems are soft and green. _____

Seed Plants

Leaves (pages 144–145)

Key Concept: **Leaves capture the sun's energy and carry out the food-making process of photosynthesis.**

- Every part of a leaf helps the leaf make food.

- Chloroplasts contain the green pigment chlorophyll. Chlorophyll traps the sun's energy to use in photosynthesis. Cells with the most chloroplasts are found near the upper surface of a leaf.

- Carbon dioxide enters a leaf through open stomata. **Stomata** (STOH muh tuh) are small openings in the surface layer of a leaf. Oxygen made during photosynthesis goes out of the leaf through the stomata.

- Water can be lost to the air through the leaves. When stomata close, they keep the plant from losing water.

Answer the following questions. Use your textbook and the ideas above.

10. Is the following sentence true or false? Leaves make food for the plant in the process of photosynthesis.

    _____

11. Circle the letter of each function of stomata.
    a. absorbing energy from the sun
    b. letting carbon dioxide enter a leaf
    c. keeping water in a leaf

Seed Plants

Gymnosperms (pages 146–150)

What Are Gymnosperms? (pages 146–147)

Key Concept: **Every gymnosperm produces naked seeds. In addition, many gymnosperms have needle-like or scalelike leaves, and deep-growing root systems.**

- A **gymnosperm** (JIM nuh spurm) is a seed plant that produces naked seeds. The seeds are naked because they are not inside a fruit. Like all seed plants, gymnosperms have vascular tissue.

- Most gymnosperms have needle-like or scalelike leaves. Gymnosperms also have roots that grow far down.

- The most common group of gymnosperms are the conifers. Conifers are gymnosperms that have cones. Pine trees are conifers.

Answer the following questions. Use your textbook and the ideas above.

1. Which is a characteristic of all gymnosperms? Circle the letter of the correct answer.
   a. naked seeds
   b. fruit
   c. shallow root systems

2. Is the following sentence true or false? Gymnosperms do not have vascular tissue. _____

3. The most common group of gymnosperms are the

   _____.

Reproduction in Gymnosperms (pages 148–149)

Key Concept: **First, pollen falls from a male cone onto a female cone. In time, a sperm cell and an egg cell join together in an ovule on the female cone.**

- In most gymnosperms, seeds form in structures called **cones**. Cones are covered with scales. Male cones produce pollen. Female cones have an egg cell at the base of each scale.

- **Pollination** is when pollen moves from the male cone to the female cone. Wind often carries pollen from male cones to female cones. Female cones are sticky so the pollen easily sticks to them.

- Once pollination occurs, the sperm cell from the pollen fertilizes the egg cell. The fertilized egg develops into the young plant inside a seed.

- When the seeds have formed, the scales of the cone open. The wind shakes the seeds out of the cone and carries them away.

Answer the following questions. Use your textbook and the ideas above.

4. Draw a line from each term to its description.

Term	Description
scale	**a.** produces pollen
	b. covers a cone
male cone	
	c. produces egg cells
female cone	

5. Which carries pollen from male cones to female cones? Circle the letter of the correct answer.

    a. wind

    b. water

    c. animals

Seed Plants

6. Complete the cycle diagram about the life cycle of gymnosperms.

Life Cycle of Gymnosperms

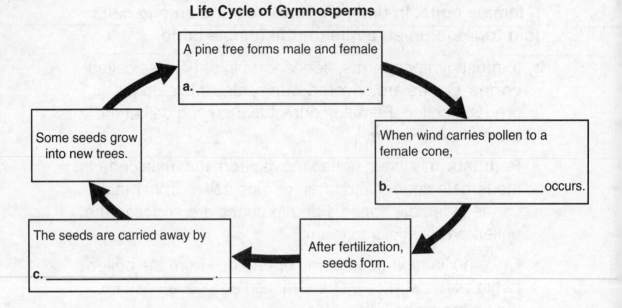

A pine tree forms male and female

a. _____ .

When wind carries pollen to a female cone,

b. _____ occurs.

After fertilization, seeds form.

The seeds are carried away by

c. _____ .

Some seeds grow into new trees.

Gymnosperms in Everyday Life (page 150)

Key Concept: **Paper and other products, such as the lumber used to build homes, come from conifers.**

- Conifers provide many useful products to people. Some products are paper, lumber, and turpentine.

- Many conifers are grown in large, managed forests. When adult trees are cut down, young trees are planted to replace them.

Answer the following question. Use your textbook and the ideas above.

7. Circle the letter of each sentence that is true about using gymnosperms.

   a. Conifers provide many useful products.

   b. Paper and turpentine come from conifers.

   c. Conifers cut from managed forests are not replaced.

Angiosperms (pages 151–157)

The Structure of Flowers (pages 152–153)

Key Concept: **All angiosperms produce flowers and seeds that are enclosed in fruits. Flowers come in all sorts of shapes, sizes, and colors. But, despite their differences, all flowers have the same function— reproduction.**

- An **angiosperm** (AN jee uh spurm) is a plant that forms seeds protected by a fruit.

- A **flower** is the structure in which seeds form. **Petals** are the colorful leaflike parts of a flower.

- Most flowers have both male and female parts.

- The **stamens** (STAY munz) are the male parts of a flower. The stamens make pollen. Pollen holds sperm cells.

- The female part of a flower is the **pistil** (PIS tul). Egg cells form in the pistil.

- The color, shape, and scent of flowers attract insects, birds, and bats. These animals pollinate flowers by moving pollen as they visit flowers to get food.

Answer the following questions. Use your textbook and the ideas above.

1. Read each word in the box. In each sentence below, fill in the correct word.

angiosperm	gymnosperm	flower

   a. The structure in which seeds form in an

      angiosperm is a(an) _____.

   b. A plant that forms seeds protected by a fruit is

      a(an) _____.

Seed Plants

2. The picture shows the parts of a flower. Label the pistil, which is the female part of the flower, and the stamens, which are the male parts of the flower.

a. _____

b. _____

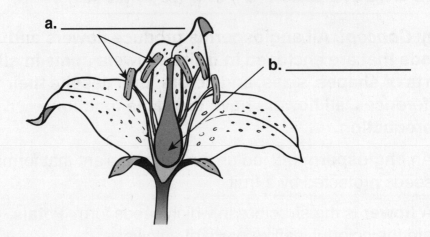

3. Insects, birds, and bats help to

_____ flowers.

Reproduction in Angiosperms (pages 154–155)

Key Concept: **Reproduction in angiosperms begins when pollen falls on a flower's stigma. In time, the sperm cell and egg cell join together in the flower's ovule. The zygote develops into the embryo part of the seed.**

- A flower is pollinated when a pollen grain falls onto the sticky top of a pistil.

- After pollination, a sperm cell from the pollen grain joins with an egg cell inside the pistil. The fertilized egg, or zygote, develops into the young plant that will be inside the seed.

- As the seed develops, part of the pistil becomes the fruit. A **fruit** contains one or more seeds.

- Fruits are a way angiosperm seeds are scattered. Animals that eat fruits spread the seeds. Other fruits are scattered by wind or water.

Seed Plants

Answer the following question. Use your textbook and the ideas on page 62.

4. Circle the letter of each sentence that is true about reproduction in angiosperms.

    a. During pollination, pollen falls onto the stamen.

    b. Part of the pistil becomes a fruit.

    c. Only wind scatters angiosperm seeds.

Types of Angiosperms (page 156)

***Key Concept:* Angiosperms are divided into two major groups: monocots and dicots.**

- "Cot" is short for *cotyledon.* Cotyledons, or seed leaves, store food used by young plants when seeds sprout.

- **Monocots** have seeds with only one seed leaf. Monocots include corn, lilies, and tulips. Monocots have flower petals in multiples of three. Their leaves are long and slender with parallel veins. Their vascular tissue is scattered throughout the stem.

- **Dicots** have seeds with two seed leaves. Some dicots are roses, oak trees, and beans. Dicot flowers have petals in multiples of four or five. Dicot leaves are wide with branching veins. Dicot stems have bundles of vascular tissue arranged in a ring.

Answer the following questions. Use your textbook and the ideas above.

5. Seeds with one seed leaf are _____.

6. Seeds with two seed leaves are _____.

Seed Plants

7. Fill in the table below to compare monocots and dicots.

Comparing Monocots and Dicots		
Plant Part	**Monocots**	**Dicots**
Leaf	a. _____ _____	branching veins
Stem	vascular tissue scattered	b. _____ _____
Flower Parts	c. _____ _____	in fours or fives

Angiosperms in Everyday Life (page 157)

Key Concept: **Angiosperms are an important source of food, clothing, and medicine for other organisms.**

- Both people and animals depend on flowering plants for food. Vegetables, fruits, grains, and grasses are all angiosperms.

- Cotton and linen clothing is made from angiosperms. Furniture is made of wood from angiosperms. Some medicines come from angiosperms.

Answer the following question. Use your textbook and the ideas above.

8. Circle the letter of each item that comes from angiosperms.
    a. clothing
    b. steel
    c. furniture

Plant Responses and Growth

(pages 160–164)

Tropisms (pages 160–161)

Key Concept: **Touch, light, and gravity are three important stimuli to which plants show growth responses, or tropisms.**

• A **tropism** (TROH piz um) is a plant's growth response toward or away from a stimulus.

• Some plants respond to touch. For example, as vines grow, they coil around any object they touch.

• Plants respond to light. The leaves, stems, and flowers of plants grow toward light. This helps a plant get the energy needed for photosynthesis.

• Plants also respond to gravity. Roots grow down into the soil, toward the pull of gravity. Stems grow up toward the sun, away from the pull of gravity.

• Plants can respond to touch, light, and gravity because they make hormones. **Hormones** are chemicals that control how plants grow and develop.

Answer the following questions. Use your textbook and the ideas above.

1. Which is a plant's response to a stimulus? Circle the letter of the correct answer.

   a. light

   b. roots growing into soil

   c. pollination

Seed Plants

2. Read each word in the box. In each sentence below, fill in the correct word.

hormone	response	tropism

a. A chemical made by a plant that controls how plants grow and develop is a

_____.

b. A plant's growth response toward or away from a stimulus is a _____.

3. Fill in the concept map about stimuli that plants respond to.

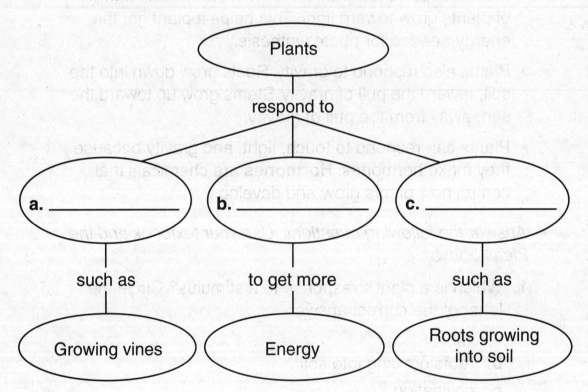

Seed Plants

Seasonal Changes (pages 162–163)

Key Concept: **The amount of darkness a plant receives determines the time of flowering in many plants. Dormancy helps plants survive freezing temperatures and the lack of liquid water.**

- Some plants flower when nights are longer. These plants usually bloom in the fall or winter. Poinsettias and chrysanthemums are two examples.

- Some plants flower when nights are shorter. These plants usually bloom in the spring or summer. Irises are an example.

- Other plants are not sensitive to the amount of darkness. Dandelions and tomatoes flower without being affected by the length of night.

- Many plants go into a state of dormancy when winter approaches. **Dormancy** is when an organism's growth or activity stops.

- A tree loses its leaves in fall. Sugars and water move into the tree's roots. Then the tree is dormant. It can survive freezing temperatures.

Answer the following questions. Use your textbook and the ideas above.

4. Circle the letter of each sentence that is true about seasonal changes.
   a. Plants that flower when nights are longer usually flower in fall or winter.
   b. All plants are sensitive to the amount of darkness.
   c. A plant stops growing during dormancy.

5. The picture shows two trees. Circle the letter of the tree that is dormant.

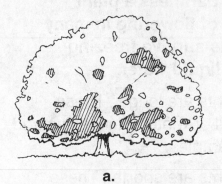 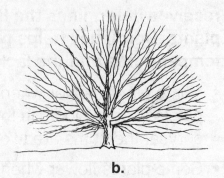

a.   b.

Life Spans of Angiosperms (page 164)

Key Concept: **Angiosperms are classified as annuals, biennials, or perennials based on the length of their life cycles.**

• **Annuals** complete a life cycle within one growing season. Marigolds and cucumbers are annuals.

• **Biennials** (by EN ee ulz) are flowering plants that complete their life cycle in two years. These plants do not flower and make seeds until the second year. Parsley is a biennial.

• **Perennials** live for more than two years. Most perennials have flowers every year. Maple trees and peonies are perennials.

Answer the following question. Use your textbook and the ideas above.

6. Draw a line from each kind of flowering plant to the length of its life cycle.

Kind of Plant	Length of Life Cycle
annual	**a.** two years
biennial	**b.** more than two years
perennial	**c.** one growing season

Feeding the World (pages 165–167)

Precision Farming (page 166)

Key Concept: **Precision farming can benefit farmers by saving time and money. It also increases crop yields by helping farmers maintain ideal conditions in all fields.**

- **Precision farming** is when farmers use only the water and fertilizer that a specific field needs.

- Satellite images of the farm fields are taken. Then a computer analyzes the images to determine the makeup of the soil. The computer makes a watering and fertilizing plan for each field.

- Precision farming saves farmers time and money. Precision farming also increases the amount of crops that are harvested.

- Precision farming is good for the environment because less fertilizer is used. There will not be extra fertilizer running off into nearby lakes and rivers.

Answer the following questions. Use your textbook and the ideas above.

1. Is the following sentence true or false? In precision farming, farmers use more water than a field needs.

   _____

2. Circle the letter of a benefit of precision farming.
   a. Fewer crops are harvested.
   b. More water is used.
   c. Less fertilizer is used.

Name _____ Date _____ Class _____

Seed Plants

3. Read the words in the box. Use the words to complete
   the flowchart to show the process of precision farming.

soil	computer	fertilizing	satellite

Precision Farming

A (An) **a.** _____ takes images of a farmer's field.

↓

A computer analyzes the images to determine the makeup of the

b. _____ in different fields on the farm.

↓

The computer prepares a watering and

c. _____ plan for each field.

Seed Plants

Hydroponics (page 166)

Key Concept: **Hydroponics allows people to grow crops in areas with poor soil to help feed a growing population.**

- **Hydroponics** (hy druh PAHN iks) is when plants are grown in solutions of nutrients instead of in soil.

- Plants are grown in containers with their roots in sand or gravel. Water with nutrients is pumped through the sand or gravel.

- Growing plants by hydroponics is expensive.

Answer the following questions. Use your textbook and the ideas above.

4. Look at the two plants. Circle the letter of the plant that is being grown by hydroponics.

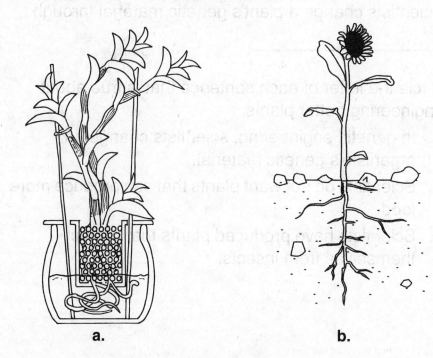

a.   b.

5. Is the following sentence true or false? The best place to use hydroponics is in areas with poor soil.

_____

Seed Plants

Engineering Better Plants (page 167)

Key Concept: **Scientists are using genetic engineering to produce plants that can grow in a wider range of climates. They are also engineering plants to be more resistant to damage from insects.**

- In **genetic engineering**, scientists change a plant's genetic material so that the plant has qualities that people find useful.

- Scientists use genetic engineering to produce plants that can grow in more climates or produce more food.

- With genetic engineering, scientists have also produced plants that can protect themselves from insects.

Answer the following questions. Use your textbook and the ideas above.

6. Scientists change a plant's genetic material through

   _____.

7. Circle the letter of each sentence that is true about engineering better plants.

   a. In genetic engineering, scientists change an organism's genetic material.

   b. Scientists do not want plants that can produce more food.

   c. Scientists have produced plants that protect themselves from insects.